Original title:
Lost in the Milky Way

Copyright © 2025 Creative Arts Management OÜ
All rights reserved.

Author: Dante Kingsley
ISBN HARDBACK: 978-1-80567-850-2
ISBN PAPERBACK: 978-1-80567-971-4

The Loneliness of the Infinite

In a vast ocean of stars, I float,
Searching for snacks, but just find a goat.
Cosmic neighbors, too busy to chat,
Wonder if they think I taste like a mat.

My telescope's broken, I see only fluff,
All this space junk, who had enough?
Aliens passed, they waved me away,
"Next time, buddy, you're in the wrong bay!"

Drifting Through Celestial Currents

Sailing on stardust, what a delight,
But my GPS says I'm out of sight.
Got lost in a wormhole, took a quick nap,
Woke with a comet, gave me a clap.

Asteroids dive like they're in a race,
Zooming past like they own the place.
I tried to join, but tripped on my boots,
Now I'm just laughing with space-cowboy flutes.

Urban Nightfall Under Cosmic Veils

City lights dimmed, I spy the void,
Lost in a crowd that can't be enjoyed.
The moon's my buddy, we play poker all night,
Joking about aliens and who's got the bite.

Traffic jams up in the Milky Blue,
Horn honking deep, but no one knew.
I asked a star for directions to Mars,
It winked and said, "I'd rather count cars!"

Celestial Pathways

Floating 'round Saturn just checking my map,
When I spotted a planet wearing a cap.
Turns out it's just space dust doing its dance,
Hoping for a twirl, not a cosmic glance.

Venus is spicy, but Pluto's just chill,
Asked for a ride, it said, "I'm not a drill."
Each star up above has a quirky trait,
Who knew the universe could be so great?

Starlight and Solitude

Twinkle toes on cosmic ground,
I dance with stars that spin around.
My spaceship's lost, oh what a sight,
   Chasing comets in the night!

Shooting stars that make a wish,
  Did I just step on a space fish?
Galaxies swirl, I trip and fall,
A jolly tumble, a space-time sprawl!

Cosmic Explorations

I packed my snacks, forgot my map,
Now I'm wedged in a Martian lap.
Conversations with an alien fry,
"Is that your spaceship? Looks like a pie!"

When asteroids bounce and planets cheer,
I sip my soda, feeling no fear.
Each black hole's a tempting prank,
I need a guide for this starry flank!

Tangled in the Celestial Tapestry

I spun a yarn of cosmic thread,
Got tangled up, now I'm misled.
My constellation shows a cat,
Pointing out to where I sat.

Zipping through the cosmic seam,
I stumbled on a gassy dream.
Jupiter laughed, said, "Stop right there!
Your rocket's caught in space-time hair!"

Twilight Over Alien Horizons

Under purple skies, I cringe and giggle,
While aliens dance, I try to jiggle.
A wormhole leads to who-knows-where,
But I'll take snacks; I have to share!

With every warp, a secret found,
I laugh at gravity spinning 'round.
As stardust rains, my worries flee,
Just me, the stars, and a cup of tea!

The Quiet Space Between

In a galaxy far, it's quite absurd,
Stars hold a meeting, not a single word.
They twinkle and jiggle, a cosmic dance,
While comets zoom by in a silly prance.

A black hole whispers, 'Keep it down, please!'
While asteroids roll like they're on a breeze.
Space bears a quiet, yet goofy charm,
As aliens giggle, not raising alarm.

The planets play poker, cards made of light,
Mars shouts 'I'm winning!' with all of his might.
Venus just flops, a confused little star,
Pluto's the dealer, he's not going far.

In this vast expanse, with chaos at play,
The universe chuckles, it's all just ballet.
So next time you stargaze, let out a grin,
For in endless space, the fun's where you've been.

When the Universe Sings

Galaxies swirl in a joyful spree,
Singing to planets like they're on TV.
Saturn spins tunes with its rings in tow,
While Earth hums softly, stealing the show.

With meteors plucking on cosmic guitars,
And black holes spinning into funky bars,
Nebulae burst forth with colors galore,
It's a star-studded party, who could ask for more?

Asteroids dance to the rhythm of space,
Floating on starlight, in a cosmic race.
Jupiter jokes with a thunderous roar,
While little green Martians just beg for more.

Cosmic confetti rains down from the moon,
Making space parties end way too soon.
So raise up a toast to this galaxy we share,
For when the universe sings, there's laughter everywhere!

Echoes of the Cosmic Ocean

Floating on cosmic waves, so grand,
Chasing comets, trying to land.
A squirrel in space with nuts to find,
Stumbling over stars, I'm quite unrefined.

Jupiter's got a giant storm, it's true,
I mistook it for my morning brew!
Sipping stardust? Don't mind if I do,
But spilled it on Mars, oh what a view!

Whispers Among the Nebulas

Nebulas giggle, they wink and they sway,
'What's that bright light? Oh, it's just Ray!'
I dance with the stars in a silly ballet,
Tripping on orbits and spinning away.

While aliens chuckle, they find me quite weird,
I waltzed with a black hole, I wasn't too steered.
"Watch your wiggle!" they chime with delight,
Gravity's pulling me left, then to right!

Drifting Through Galactic Dreams

In a dreamscape of twinkling delight,
Jumping from meteor to moonlight.
A wormhole opened, threw me for a spin,
Thought I'd lost count of the stars in my win!

I tango with stardust, what a great sight,
But fell through a planet—landed in fright!
"Oh dear," I said, "this isn't on track,"
Out pops a T-Rex, 'Hey, want your hat back?'

Stellar Shadows

Galaxies giggle in a dark, dreamy haze,
I fumble and tumble through cosmic maze.
Starshine and giggles fill up the night,
Bumping into Saturn, what a silly fright!

Meteor showers raining down like confetti,
I thought it was candy; my taste buds weren't ready.
Pluto called out, 'Hey, wanna come play?'
So we danced in shadows till the break of day!

The Stillness of the Infinite

Stars dance in the void, quite a sight,
While I trip on stardust, what a night!
Planets giggle as they spin around,
I'd wave, but I've lost my space-bound ground.

Asteroids whizz by with silly tunes,
Singing, 'Come join us, you silly, loon!'
Black holes chuckle, hiding their snack,
'One more traveler, and we'll take them back!'

Weightless in the Dark

Floating like a feather, what a thrill,
Lost my puffer coat, I feel the chill.
Gravity forgot me in this expanse,
Space is a party, come join the dance!

Astro-critters juggling moons in cheer,
I shout, 'Save some stars for me over here!'
Silent giggles echo, sweet and bright,
While I drift along, what a silly plight!

The Constellation's Lament

Up above, the stars start to feud,
Drawing lines between their mood,
'I'm a bear!' one declares with flair,
While the others say, 'You're just a chair!'

Twirling nebulae shake their dust,
'We need a committee to settle this fuss!'
But comets swoop in with their tails all a-blur,
'Let's just eat space pie and forget the stir!'

Bouncing between the Celestial Bodies

I bounce from star to star, quite a sight,
Each landing is wobbly, oh what a fright!
Jupiter trips me, Saturn gives chase,
'Catch me if you can!' in this cosmic race!

Galaxies swirl, they tease and they poke,
'You call that a jump? Man, that's a joke!'
Laughter echoes through the endless night,
As I tumble and roll, what a giggly flight!

Transcending Cosmic Boundaries

A spaceship made of cheese, it flies,
Past twinkling stars and glowing pies.
The captain's hat is just a cap,
He steers with snacks, what a silly chap!

In orbit 'round a giant moon,
They dance to a peculiar tune.
With marshmallow rockets, they zip and zoom,
While space cows graze in cosmic gloom.

Asteroids made of chocolate chips,
They dodge them with their wibble-wobble quips.
The universe uncorks a giggly cheer,
As cosmic critters join in the beer!

With galaxies swirling in a spin,
They laugh at time, it's a real win.
In this absurd celestial play,
They munch on stardust, come what may!

The Drift of Endless Night

Out in the dark where shadows lie,
A space cat yawns and gives a sigh.
It pounces on a comet's tail,
And giggles as it starts to sail.

Floating through a nebula's mess,
A sloth in a space suit starts to dress.
With glitter glue and lots of flair,
They twirl like planets without a care!

Starry fish swim in the vacuum air,
Their scales are bright, their laughter rare.
They play with beams of blinding light,
While chasing moons, oh what a sight!

When space hiccups, and stardust falls,
They bounce around like cosmic balls.
With every giggle, the cosmos sways,
In this drift of endless, silly ways!

Fading into the Cosmic Whisper

Whispers float from black holes wide,
"Did you pack snacks?" they seem to chide.
A donut ship glides with a grin,
Its crew just wants to dive right in!

The stars can't help but crack a joke,
As comets trail a sweet smoke.
A space llama hums a tune,
While dodging a late, runaway balloon.

Tiny aliens dance on Mars,
Dressed up like glittery space cars.
They trip on rings of Saturn's grace,
Spinning 'round like a silly race!

Through cosmic laughter, they drift and sway,
In a universe that's here to play.
With every giggle, they light the night,
Fading soft in a galactic delight!

Celestial Marauders

Once upon a shooting star,
A band of pirates sailed afar.
With bags of chips and fizzy drinks,
They plotted heists with crazy winks.

They raid the rings of Saturn's glow,
Stealing sparkles and comic shows.
With telescopes, they search for gold,
But find just socks and stories bold!

Galactic pranks are their main game,
At every planet, they stake their claim.
A gassy giant joins the fun,
While bursting bubbles—one by one!

As starlight twirls in cosmic beams,
These merry marauders chase their dreams.
In the vastness, they roar with glee,
For space is wild, as wild can be!

Journey Through Celestial Echoes

The stars are giggling, what a sight,
They're playing tag in the endless night.
A comet sneezed, oh what a mess,
Galactic dust adds to our dress.

A space cow bounces, oh what fun,
While aliens dance, they're number one.
Meteorite races, a two-star team,
Chasing dreams in a cosmic beam.

Black holes whisper jokes, what a treat,
The silence breaks with a raucous beat.
Asteroids laugh, in a silly show,
Floating around with a spin and a glow.

So grab your friends, let's play up here,
In this vast circus, oh so dear.
Each twinkling laugh and swirling spin,
Is where the universe truly begins.

Waking in the Universe's Embrace

I woke up sideways on a moonlit beam,
Dreaming of tacos, or so it would seem.
Stars wink at me, like they've had too much,
A cosmic party, I feel their touch.

Alien chefs serve interstellar pies,
With toppings made from alien fries.
Gravity's playing funny tricks,
As I dodge planets doing sweet flips.

The sun's a huge smile, shining bright,
While planets groove through cosmic plight.
I trip on stardust, then roll in glee,
This universe dances, wild and free.

Floating through wonders, I chuckle aloud,
In the arms of the sky, I'm feeling proud.
So here's to the laughter, the joy we share,
In the grand embrace of the cosmic air.

Floating Among the Starborn

I floated past a starry snack stand,
With cosmic chips and a soda so grand.
Galaxies bubble with sweet delight,
As I feast on starlight, my kinda night.

A comet offered rides on shiny trails,
While space-fish sang their lovely tales.
I waved to the aliens, such good buds,
In their zany rocket, we splashed through floods.

Moon bunnies hop in their silver suits,
A dance-off starts with flapping boots.
The rocket zooms in a dizzying whirl,
As space giggles make my head twirl.

Life in the stars is a marvelous spree,
With laughter echoing, one, two, three.
So grab your friends and smile away,
In this bright, wild, and funny celestial play.

The Cosmic In-Between

In the cosmic in-between, where wonders collide,
Jellybean planets were bouncing with pride.
Shooting stars raced, their tails in a spin,
Winking at stardust, inviting a grin.

I met a black cat with glowing green eyes,
Juggling moon rocks while sharing big pies.
He told me of sights that twist and unfold,
In the funny space tales that never get old.

Space cows on hoverboards slide through the air,
While robots do the cha-cha without a care.
The universe chuckles, a giggling spree,
In this wacky expanse, so wild and free.

So let's toast with comets, and dance on a beam,
Join the road trip on this cosmic dream.
With laughter and joy drawn across the sky,
The in-between's where we fly high.

A Journey through Starlit Dreams

Sailing through stars on a marshmallow boat,
Dodging those comets while munching a oat.
Jellybean clouds give a bounce to our flight,
Whispers of giggles float by in the night.

Aliens wave from their candy cane homes,
Offering snacks from their fizzy star foams.
With laughter and joy, we twirl in the breeze,
Dancing with light beams and cosmic whirlpools, please!

Galactic confetti bursts under our feet,
Making wishes pop like a sugary treat.
We cartwheel past planets that wobbly spin,
With each spin a chuckle, we dive right in.

Bouncing on moons like they're trampolines,
Under doodle-sky paintings of whimsical scenes.
In starlit dreams, the fun never ends,
Join this wild ride, where silliness blends!

The Infinite Night's Embrace

In the cosmic sea, we surf on a ray,
Chasing our shadows, we giggle and play.
Shooting through starfields like candy on sticks,
Finding new constellations of quirky antics.

With giggles and gaffes, we dance through the dark,
Each supernova a bright little spark.
Navigating laughter through quirky space trails,
Loopy space llamas in comet-tailingails!

Wobbling planets smile wide as they spin,
With sparkly grins, they invite us right in.
We play hopscotch on Saturn's bright rings,
While ducks in bow ties serenade us with sings.

Stars wear sombreros on festival nights,
And marathon meteors display their slick lights.
In this zany expanse with joy as our guide,
We take a big leap, in laughter we glide!

Among Celestial Shadows

Floating through darkness where jellybeans shine,
Planning a party with old friends of mine.
Whirling around in a sparkling spree,
Hoping that aliens will join in with glee.

Stars twinkle secrets with giggles galore,
Whiskeys made of stardust and lemonade pour.
While moons do a jig, showing off their new dance,
We chuckle at meteors, giving us a chance.

Cosmic popcorn pops under our feet,
With sour space juice that's delicious to eat.
Navigating shadows of floating space pies,
While rockets and critters shoot candy from skies.

In comical orbits around funny-faced suns,
We play leapfrog with comets, oh what endless fun!
Our laughter rings out through this celestial place,
In shadows of wonders, we forever embrace.

Navigating the Nebula's Heart

We spin through the nebula, chasing our tails,
With cotton candy dolphins and moonbeam gales.
Each puddle of stardust brings giggles and cheer,
Silly sparks flying, nothing to fear!

Playing hide and seek in this colorful haze,
While twinkling stars chuckle in brilliant displays.
A hop on a comet, with friends we unite,
In the heart of the nebula, a wacky delight.

Pizza-shaped asteroids float by with some flair,
And unicorn astronauts rock the great air.
With jellylike planets that twist and that sway,
Surprises await us, come join the buffet!

We laugh with the galaxies, spreading good vibes,
Finding fun moments that everyone bribes.
In the heartbeat of space where the laughter reveals,
Navigating the nebula spins endless appeals!

Celestial Footprints

In galaxies where socks disappear,
The stars play hide and seek in cheer.
Comets zoom with a fizz and pop,
While aliens tease, "You'll never stop!"

Moonbeams tickle this astronaut's nose,
As rockets launch from cosmic prose.
Floating past planets, a cosmic prank,
A satellite giggles, 'We're on the flank!'

Meteor showers bring sprinkles of fun,
Chasing stardust on the cosmic run.
Laughter echoes from worlds unexplored,
We dance among nebulas, feeling adored!

Jupiter's storms roll with jolly glee,
Saturn's rings jingle, as happy as can be.
Through this galactic carnival's sway,
Who knew space was a game we could play?

The Astral Wonderlust

I packed my bags with space snacks galore,
To journey through stars I can't ignore.
With gummy comets and licorice moons,
I set off to dance with the cosmic tunes.

A UFO zooms by, 'Hey, what's your deal?'
I shrug and reply, 'I'm just here for the meal!'
Planets laugh as I twirl and glide,
In this vast playground, I take great pride.

Black holes grin with a mischievous stare,
I wink back, 'You can't take my hair!'
Galaxies spin like tops in the sky,
While I munch on stardust, oh my, oh my!

Floating past supernovas and their shine,
With each burst of light, I sip on some wine.
Who knew the cosmos could party this way?
Now every night feels like a holiday!

Echoes from the Spiral Arms

In a spiral dance, stars whirl and spin,
Cosmic confetti falls, let the fun begin!
A pulsar beeps its catchy refrain,
While shooting stars fuel our silly game.

Why did the nebula cross the void?
To get to the other side, oh boy!
Planets roll out the red carpet gleam,
As we slide down the Milky Way stream.

Whispers float from asteroids nearby,
'Want to catch a ride? We can fly high!'
In spacesuits bright with colors that clash,
Laughter erupts with every wild splash.

Cosmic jokes light up the endless night,
As we giggle at gravity's silly plight.
In this stellar playground, we all play along,
Echoes of giggles, where we all belong!

Beneath a Canopy of Stars

Beneath the stars, I spread my mat,
Unicorns dance, and I chat with the cat.
A meteor asks, 'Want to sip onshine?'
We share giggles under the starry line.

Constellations wink, as if in on the joke,
'Watch out for aliens, they're prone to croak!'
With a telescope, I spy on the spree,
Comets throw a rave, come join the glee!

Mars throws a party, with snacks on deck,
While Venus grins, what the heck?
In a dizzy daze, we all spin around,
Getting lost in laughter, our joy knows no bounds.

So here we float, in a night full of mirth,
Where comedy thrives amidst cosmic birth.
Under canvas bright, we laugh and we play,
Chasing our dreams in a wacky ballet!

Timeless Whispers of the Nebula

Stars are twinkling, oh so bright,
Aliens may join the dance tonight.
A cosmic joke in endless flight,
Space snacks floating, what a sight!

Asteroids bump with a clumsy flair,
Planets wobble, flipping in air.
Don't ask why, no one seems to care,
Just laugh with stardust, if you dare!

Gravity's lost its sense of fun,
Spinning 'round like a chuckling sun.
Comets race, watch them run,
In the cosmos, we all have won!

So let's toast to the stars above,
With goofy grins and cosmic love.
For in this vast, whimsical glove,
We're all just kids, the universe our playground glove.

Fractured Horizons

Galaxies giggle in the night,
Playing tag, a hilarious sight.
Supernovas burst with delight,
While Saturn's rings keep rolling tight.

Black holes spin with mysterious flair,
Sucking in laughter from everywhere.
What's that noise? Oh, balloons in air!
Just cosmic parties we all can share.

Astro-dogs chase the glowing trails,
On shooting stars, they share their tales.
Nebulous kites do playful flails,
Universe's laughter never fails!

So here's to the quirks in space's grasp,
With vibrant colors and cosmic rasp.
Join the fun, it's an epic clasp,
In fractured horizons, let's all gasp!

Glimmers of the Farthest Reach

Winks from Venus, a cheeky glow,
Clouds of mischief start to grow.
Galactic tickles to and fro,
As comets play, 'Hey, watch me throw!'

Mars chuckles, with a dusty grin,
While Jupiter joins in, letting the fun begin.
"Let's race to the moons!" they spin,
In the cosmic frolic, where all are kin!

These twinkling lights dance with glee,
While space whales sing harmoniously.
Glimmers of laughter, wild and free,
In this vast realm of jubilee!

Snap your fingers, count to three,
Join the laughter, if you agree.
Cosmic pranks are guaranteed,
In the farthest reaches, let's all be!

A Dance in the Emptiness

In the void where nothing's found,
Stars go 'zoom' with a whirly sound.
Space-beings twirl, round and round,
While meteor showers crash the ground!

Orbiting giggles fill the air,
With black holes playing truth or dare.
"Catch my light!" the quasars declare,
In this vast expanse, we all share.

With cosmic hats and sparkly shoes,
Dancing to a beat of vibrant hues.
The starlit hide-and-seek ensues,
And gravity laughs, it just can't lose!

So float away on joy's embrace,
In this funny, grand, vast space.
Join the dance, quicken your pace,
In the emptiness, we find our place!

Shimmering Void

In the vastness where stars play,
I dressed up as a comet today.
But I tripped on a cosmic ray,
And now I'm floating—hip hooray!

I asked a black hole for the way,
It just gulped me without delay.
Spinning through space in ballet,
My dance is bold, come join the fray!

Planets laugh, they twirl and sway,
While I chase my tail, oh what a day!
Asteroids shout, 'Hey, don't decay!'
As I wave goodbye—bye-bye, okay?

In this void, I'm the clown at play,
With sparkles and giggles on display.
So if you see me, don't dismay,
I'm just a joke in the Milky Bay!

Shadows of Ancient Light

In the depth of night, stars ignite,
Casting shadows, oh what a sight!
I told my buddy, 'Take a bite,'
Of cosmic fruit—what pure delight!

But he mistook a meteorite,
And said, 'This snack feels just too tight!'
While comets chuckled, shining bright,
We danced 'neath the beams of starlight.

The Martians peeked, with their eyes white,
Laughing as we put on our flight.
An intergalactic karaoke night,
Oh how we sang under celestial height!

With each shadow, there's fun in sight,
Exploring dark with hearts so light.
Together we'll drift, out of spite,
Becoming legends in the moonlight!

The Lost Compass of the Cosmos

I found a compass, much to my joy,
But it pointed wrong—oh what a ploy!
It led me in circles, like a toy,
Now I'm the star of my own parody!

I asked Orion where to go,
He winked and said, "Just steal the show!"
While galaxies laughed in a row,
I pirouetted like a cosmic pro!

The bears above think I'm in woe,
But I'm just lost in this vibrant flow.
Chasing stars, swaying to the tempo,
Of the universe's wacky lingo!

With my compass, we're friends in tow,
Together we skip, we leap, we glow.
In this folly, I'll make it so,
That cosmic mischief is the way to go!

Galactic Farewell

As the stars wave their bright goodbye,
I'm loading my spaceship, oh my, oh my!
With snacks packed tight, I start to fly,
    Waving to aliens that drift by.

The sun gave a wink, a fiery sigh,
While the moons danced close, oh why, oh why?
I swallowed hard, and let out a cry,
"Who knew space travel would make me shy?"

Pulsars flashing like a strobe light,
I giggled at time, what a fright!
Each tick a joke in the cosmic night,
As I soared through the twinkling height.

So here's my tale of a galactic flight,
With laughter and fun, my heart feels light.
I bid adieu to the starry sight,
In this funny space, all feels right!

Dreaming Under Cosmic Canopies

Under twinkling lights on high,
I wondered why the aliens spy.
Do they take notes on human quirks?
Or just giggle at our silly works?

A comet tail, a wobbly dance,
While Pluto throws a retro chance.
I tried to catch a shooting star,
But ended up in a cosmic bar!

Bouncing off the moons with glee,
I spilled my drink on gravity.
The Martians laughed, they shared a toast,
To Earthlings lost in their own boast!

With jelly beans from Saturn's ring,
I dream of trips on plucky springs.
In the vastness, we just play,
As comets chuckle on their way.

Starlit Desolation

Floating high in starry void,
I thought I'd find a friend or droid.
But all I heard were cosmic sighs,
And echoes of forgotten pies!

The space cows moo in zero G,
With moon cheese for their jubilee.
I asked for milk, they gave a laugh,
Said, 'Why not try the starlight half?'

Drifting past a nebula's haze,
I tripped on space-tape in a daze.
The rocket raccoons had a feast,
Of intergalactic peanut butter at least!

With twinkling stars as my lanterns bright,
I navigated through the cosmic night.
Though desolation brought some fright,
I found my joy in the quirky light.

Cosmic Footprints

In the dust of ancient moons I tread,
Finding footprints that once led.
Who played hopscotch on Mars' face?
I see the marks of an alien race!

Backwards footsteps on the comet's tail,
A UFO driver who turned pale.
"Where's Earth?" he cried with a pizza slice,
"Did I miss the turn? Oh, that's not nice!"

Space ducks quack and waddle slow,
In a interstellar cosmic show.
With a map made of spaghetti strands,
I wander through enchanted bands.

The footprints lead to a cosmic fair,
With cotton candy floating in the air.
I joined the dance, we spun and twirled,
What a wild night in this strange world!

A Song of Wandering Stars

Oh, sing to me, you playful lights,
Who jive with comets through the nights.
Do you hum tunes of ancient lore,
Or crash into each other, wanting more?

A galaxy choir, they sound so grand,
With harmony that's hard to understand.
They twinkle jokes with every flare,
And crack up the void, with cosmic flair!

With every wink, they tell a tale,
Of wandering ships that set the sail.
While meteors chase a dream so bright,
They dance through the chaos of endless flight!

So pass the snacks, we'll laugh till dawn,
As stars keep shining, and spaces yawn.
With a twinkle in their gleaming hearts,
These cheeky gems will never part.

The Galactic Odyssey

In a rocket made of cheese,
I zoom past starry trees.
An alien waves with a grin,
Saying, "Care for some space gin?"

Asteroids dance in silly rounds,
As comets play joyful sounds.
I trip on a flying squid,
And laugh till my sides are hid.

Space cows munch on moonlight grass,
While I zoom by at quite the class.
They tip their hats with a moo,
As if they know just what to do.

My GPS says 'Go ahead!'
But points me back to my own bed.
I guess I'd better steer this ship,
Before I find an alien trip.

Fragments of Distant Light

Stars wink and giggle afar,
One tried to start a rock band, bizarre.
Pluto sent a sparkly note,
Saying, "Join us? Bring your coat!"

The sun's a great big glowing ball,
But he just wants to play squash and sprawl.
With each creation and supernova,
I try to dodge a galactic sofa.

A black hole's sucking in my snack,
I yell, "Hey, bring that boomerang back!"
Supernovae pop like popcorn,
While I wear this space hat, well-worn.

Floating on a cosmic bike,
I whirl around, just for a hike.
But tripping on a starry trail,
I giggle, saying, "Oops! No email!"

Beneath the Cosmic Canopy

Underneath the starry quilt,
I found a comet made of silt.
It told me tales of cosmic tricks,
While space mice played on space bricks.

Nebulas brewing funky stew,
And dancing planets, quite the crew.
I questioned why the moon won't shine,
She grinned and said, "I'm out of line!"

Each star wears a quirky mask,
As if they're all on a fun task.
The cosmos sings a silly tune,
While meteor showers dance at noon.

I tried to catch a shooting star,
But it flew off to a distant bar.
Guess I'll stick with my light drink,
And plan a space trip, don't you think?

Shadows of the Stellar Sea

In the vastness of space, I roam,
Chasing shadows far from home.
A thrifty astronaut on a spree,
Catching starlight for my tea.

A playful ghost from a distant sun,
Told me jokes, oh what fun!
While dark matter floats in a swirl,
Making me feel like a silly girl.

Gravity's pulling a prank on me,
As I float and sip on honey tea.
I peek through a wormhole's door,
And end up on a candy shore.

The Milky Way giggles with delight,
As I dance through the cosmic night.
With a wink and wave, I sashay,
Shadows whisper, 'What a day!'

Cradled by Starlight

Twinkling lights dance in the sky,
I tripped on a comet, oh my!
Floating marshmallows, I swear,
Shooting stars whisper, "No fair!"

Space squirrels giggle, take a peek,
They play hide and seek, so sleek.
On a ring of Saturn, I spin,
Chasing dreams with a goofy grin.

Galaxies chuckle, what a scene,
Rocket raccoons, wearing green.
They tell me jokes about black holes,
I'm chuckling, losing control!

In this cosmic circus, I play,
With balloons shaped like the Milky Way.
What a ride, so silly and bright,
Cradled softly by starlight tonight.

The Forgotten Starship

Once I flew on a rusting ship,
Dodging asteroids with a funny flip.
Pilot said, "Is that a bird?"
It was just my sandwich, absurd!

Mechanical mice ran loose inside,
Stealing snacks, they did not hide.
In the cargo bay, a dance-off sparked,
Even the engines joined, remark!

Planets waved, "Come take a ride!"
But my ship was stuck, I just sighed.
Found a glitch that sent us up,
Now we're sipping cosmic cup!

The stars snicker as we drift,
My ship's a joke, but such a gift.
Floating with laughter, not a care,
In this wild, stellar affair.

Moonlit Pilgrimage

On a quest for alien snacks,
I wore socks with silly hacks.
Through lunar craters, I proudly prance,
My space boots squeak, what a chance!

Stumbling over moonlit dust,
I tripped on my own cosmic trust.
A diary full of jiggly dreams,
And wobbly paths bursting at the seams.

Found a garden of giggling stars,
They told me secrets from afar.
"Don't eat the rocks!" they all warned,
But I chomped one—oh, I'm adorned!

With glimmering crumbs on my face,
I laugh as I float, a joyful grace.
Voyaging wild, through night so bright,
A pilgrimage wrapped in delight.

Embrace of the Astral Unknown

Into the void, I took a leap,
Did I pack snacks? Not a peep.
Floating freely, I fetch for fun,
A space cat dances, on the run!

Galactic grapes roll around,
I fumble, my balance unbound.
With cosmic friends, we play charades,
In the stardust of cosmic parades.

Lunar giraffes stretch to the sky,
"Do they drink tea?" I wonder why.
Jellybean meteors bounce with flair,
In this wacky, starry fair!

Embraced by the quirks of the night,
Every twist a giggle, pure delight.
With whims of the universe as my guide,
In the embrace of the astral, I glide!

Trails of Stardust Memories

Floating donuts in the night,
Caffeine dreams take flight.
Tangled in a web of light,
I tripped on stars, what a sight!

Galactic hiccups, cosmic fries,
Orbiting thoughts that might surprise.
Aliens dance, oh such wise pies,
With a wink, they steal the skies!

Supernova snacks, a tasty treat,
Asteroids roll, can't find my seat.
Laughter echoes, a comical beat,
In this space, life's still sweet!

Leprechauns hiding near black holes,
Playing jokes on wandering souls.
I shouted, "Hey! I'm on a roll!"
The universe giggled, that's how it unfolds!

Wanderlust Among the Stars

Galaxies twirl like cotton candy,
Cosmic travel, it's quite dandy.
Snapped a selfie, with Martian Brandy,
Thought I was clever, but it looks handy!

Shooting stars on a pizza slice,
Every bite proves it's quite nice.
Gravity pulls, ain't that a spice?
Floating high, avoiding the mice!

Nebulae sprouting like wildflowers,
I tried to hug them, I had the powers.
But they giggled, "We're a bit sour!"
To which I laughed, "Give me the hours!"

Pulsars poke with a joke or two,
Dancing comets, all in queue.
Chasing laughter through the blue,
In this space, fun always ensues!

The Silent Sprawl of the Universe

Space is big, I lost my shoes,
Tripping over cosmic blues.
Planets gossip, news they enthuse,
While I'm here, just stuck with snooze!

Black holes munch like hungry teens,
Sucking in all my memes.
Starlit pranks fill the scenes,
With goofy aliens and their schemes!

Superstars strut in golden capes,
Making fun of all my shapes.
I pretend to be wise, like the apes,
But in this void, it's just scrapes!

Wormholes wink with a cheeky tease,
Whispering secrets, bending knees.
"Come join us for interstellar ease,"
I laughed and took the cosmic breeze!

Nebulous Heartbeats

In the nebulous dance, I found my stride,
With glittering trails, I can't hide.
Stars give me a cosmic ride,
While quasars laugh, oh what a tide!

Meteor showers held a rave,
With space critters dancing brave.
I brought cookies, but they gave me a wave,
As they spun around, oh how I crave!

Celestial giggles tickle my ears,
While planets toast to springtime cheers.
Vortex of fun pulls me near,
In this galaxy, I've got no fears!

Floating through whims of orb-like tunes,
Cosmic pranks amid the dunes.
Riding waves of laughter, it balloons,
As I jive under the light of moons!

Journey to the Edge of Light

A spaceship made of cheese and bread,
With silly stars above our head.
We zoom past planets dressed in hats,
Dodging space cats and cosmic bats.

The moon just winked, it's quite a tease,
While Mars wore shoes, if you please.
Asteroids dance like they're at a ball,
And we just giggle, having a ball!

Jupiter's storm, oh what a show,
While Saturn spins a hula-hoop glow.
We laugh and munch on comet treats,
Space travel's fun, it's hard to beat!

With light-years wrapped in a goofy rhyme,
We bounce through space, oh what a time!
Galaxies twirl in a swirling ballet,
We'll party 'til dawn, in a light-speed sway.

Reveries in the Cosmic Void

In a black hole, I lost a shoe,
Now I dance with stars as my crew.
We twirl through nebulas dressed in spark,
Making shadows that sing in the dark.

Asteroids argue in silly debates,
While Venus just laughs and bakes cosmic cakes.
Galactic giggles echo in space,
With comets zipping like they're in a race!

Aliens pop up, with antennas and grins,
"Join us for snacks and some stellar spins!"
They juggle moon rocks with effortless flair,
While quasars giggle, floating in air.

The universe hums a playful tune,
While I dance with a star and a cartoon.
Dreams swirl like galaxies near and far,
In this wonky, whimsical cosmic bazaar!

Lullabies of the Celestial Sphere

The sun sings softly, a lullaby bright,
While Saturn's rings twinkle in the night.
Stars yawn and stretch in a cosmic bed,
As meteors dance, their wishes widespread.

Galaxies cuddle in a swirling embrace,
While comets tickle the vast, open space.
A nebula whispers, "Sleep tight, my dear,"
As we float in dreams, without a fear.

Twinkle light-years, counting up sheep,
While black holes hum us deep into sleep.
The universe whispers, "Let's drift away,"
In a cozy, celestial cabaret.

Meteors rush by with a giggle and cheer,
As they play peek-a-boo, bringing us near.
Starlight cradles us softly, it seems,
In this playful galaxy woven from dreams.

The Starlit Maze

In a maze of stars, I twirl and spin,
Trying to find the way to begin.
Each corner I turn brings a burst of light,
With giggles echoing through the night.

A shooting star races, "Catch me if you can!"
But I trip over a stardust span.
Through wormholes that wiggle and bubble with glee,
"Oops! Not that way!" calls a lost galaxy.

Space-time ties make a messy old knot,
While quirky quasars shine brightly on the spot.
Planets play tag, with a bounce and a leap,
This cosmic adventure is quite the sweep!

With each twist and turn, laughter abounds,
As I dance through rings, spinning round and round.
In the starlit maze, it's a whimsical race,
Where the universe smiles and embraces my face!

Constellation Dreams

In the night, I drift so high,
Chasing stars that twinkle by.
They giggle as they hide away,
Playing games of cosmic sway.

I thought I saw a sandwich there,
With moon cheese, it gave me a glare.
But as I reached for that delight,
It turned to dust in sparkly flight.

My friends, the comets, zoomed on by,
Waving tails, they made me sigh.
A cosmic dance, we all partake,
Oh, the moves we'll never make!

Floating past a planet's bags,
Oh look! A thrift store where it hangs!
With shiny rocks and spacey clothes,
I shopped for things that no one knows.

The Stellar Sojourn

Rocket fuel made of jelly beans,
I drift through dreams, or so it seems.
Giant ducks in space parade,
With rubber boots, they serenade.

I asked the sun for a selfie shot,
He scratched his head and said, 'Why not?'
We posed beside a cosmic pie,
A slice of joy; oh my, oh my!

Jupiter served up stardust fries,
With a side of asteroids in disguise.
I danced with stars, all shiny bright,
While Saturn laughed, "What a sight!"

I tried to land on Mars but tripped,
And ended up in Venus' script.
There, planets giggled, spinning 'round,
A silly cosmic merry-go-round.

Celestial Wanderers

Around the stars we twirl and spin,
Catching tales of where we've been.
Cosmic jesters with hearts so quick,
In a universe that's quite the trick!

A moonbeams' cat chased comets' dreams,
Tying them up in laughter streams.
They swung on rings of icy grace,
While we joined that wild space race!

Neptune's blues wore a frown so deep,
But I offered him a joke to keep.
He chuckled loud, the cosmos shook,
And suddenly, his mood just took!

In a snack bar made of cosmic gas,
We feasted on the stars, oh what a class!
But when I took a bite, what a mess,
With giggles echoing, I must confess!

Starlit Labyrinth

In a maze of twinkling dots,
I ran in circles, hit the spots.
With a grin, a star said, "What's the rush?"
I laughed and danced in a cosmic hush.

Bumping into a galactic wall,
I asked a comet, "Had enough fun?"
With a wink, it dashed, said, "Not at all!"
And off it went, on the stellar run.

Chasing light through swirling beams,
Wishing to hop on starlit dreams.
Every corner held a cheeky tease,
With winking planets—what a breeze!

Eventually, I tripped on a star,
"Excuse me!" I laughed, "Where you going far?"
It twirled away, a celestial prank,
I stood there giggling, my heart full of thanks.

A Journey Beyond Familiar Skies

I took my cat on a space ride,
She wore a helmet, I could not hide.
Floating snacks made her paws go spry,
We shared a laugh as we zoomed by.

Stars wiggled like jelly, what a sight,
They giggled back; oh what pure delight.
We danced around planets, chased comets too,
What a fun party with a galactic crew!

But the cat got dizzy, wobbled and spun,
Adjourned our tour, declared it was done.
With a purr and a yawn, she curled for a nap,
While I floated blissfully, tasting the gap.

In this stretch of space where the asteroids drift,
We find cosmic mischief, the ultimate gift.
Each twinkle above, a chuckle to share,
In our zany ship, we float without care.

Distant Echoes of Lost Worlds

I dialed the stars on an old radio,
Hoping to find where the wild things go.
A voice crackled back, said, "Don't you dare!"
I laughed so hard, it bounced off the air.

The planets were busy, they never look down,
Spinning like tops in a cosmic town.
I asked them for tea, they laughed out loud,
"Not now, we're busy, come join the crowd!"

Saturn wore rings, like a fashion faux pas,
He winked and twirled, oh what a bizarre!
Venus brought cupcakes, but they were all dry,
We spat out the crumbs, it was worth the try.

As the stars played tag, I shouted with glee,
In this wild playground, we danced all free.
Past horizons of laughter, I could see the way,
To the echo of worlds that just love to play.

Seeking the Aurora of the Unknown

With rocket boots on, I floated away,
Chasing a rainbow, what a wild display!
The galaxies chuckled, igniting a swirl,
As cosmic confetti danced all in a whirl.

I asked a black hole for secrets so grand,
It only replied with a not-so-gentle hand.
I tumbled and twirled, kissed by wild space winds,
That's when I knew, I'm losing my pins!

Electric sprites from the nebula wiped,
Tickling my toes, feeling quite hyped.
With giggles and gasps, we hopped star to star,
I felt like a hero, a cosmic bazaar!

But then the Auroras, they played hard to get,
Zipping and zooming, oh what a threat!
I laughed and I chased through the shimmering hue,
In this silly pursuit, the fun just grew.

The Allure of Celestial Abyss

I peeked in a void, it blinked right at me,
Whispered some secrets not meant to be free.
With every quasar that popped up to greet,
I snickered and wondered, what a lively treat!

Asteroids threw parties in infinite space,
Cake made of stardust, what a dreamy place!
I tried to join in, but they spun me around,
I landed on Pluto, lost in the sound.

Comets invited, with trails made of light,
"Dance on our glitter, come join the flight!"
I twirled and I spun, at last feeling bold,
In the cosmic ballet, I laughed till I rolled.

Beneath cosmic laughter, I found my delight,
In the depths of the void, a whimsical sight.
So here in the abyss, I'll twirl every day,
Chasing the allure while I laugh all the way.

A Dance Among the Stars

Under the glow of a neon moon,
We twirl and spin with a cosmic boon.
Aliens watch with gaping grins,
As we trip over our starry fins.

Comets pass with a whoosh and cheer,
They laugh at us, but we persevere.
Asteroids join in the jiving fun,
Making us believe we've just begun.

Black holes wink in the darkened sky,
Whispering secrets as we pass by.
We dance on the edge of a planetary stage,
In a ballet of quirks at every age.

So grab a moonbeam, let's take a chance,
With the universe, we'll happily prance.
For in this galaxy, we feel so free,
Come, join the fun, and dance with me!

Adrift in the Cosmic Sea

Sailing through stars on a marshmallow boat,
With gummy bears serving as our float.
Asteroids bounce, oh what a sight,
As we giggle and drift on this galactic night.

Space whales sing tunes from far-off worlds,
While candy comets leave trails that swirled.
We swish and swoosh, like a cosmic kite,
In this bubble of sweetness and pure delight.

Planets throw parties, we crash with glee,
Bouncing on rings of a jovial spree.
Feet on the ground, but hearts in the sky,
In a pirate ship ready to fly.

So let's toast our sodas to the grand abyss,
In a universe where we find our bliss.
With laughter as bubbles floating away,
We sing in joy, adrift in play!

Galaxies of Forgotten Thoughts

Amidst the stars, ideas go to sleep,
Like dusty books piled in a cosmic heap.
We rummage through nebulas, what a trip,
Finding old doodles on a starry slip.

Memories swirl like glittery dust,
A cat thinks deeply, as cats often must.
We chase after echoes of laughter's past,
In this galaxy, the fun's built to last.

Thoughts float by in a colorful dance,
We giggle at each whimsical glance.
With martian jokes and lunar glee,
Our minds are afloat in this strange spree.

So come aboard, let's take this ride,
Through a cosmic mosaic, where dreams collide.
In galaxies wide, we'll cuddle the whims,
With smiles that twinkle and joy that brims!

Ephemeral Constellations

Under a canopy of glimmering tales,
Shooting stars skitter like fish with scales.
We pick constellations like space-fried snacks,
Using our dreams as playful tracks.

A bear and a maiden dance through the night,
Jumping and jiving with pure delight.
With upturned faces and eyes like the sky,
We chase after wonders, oh my, oh my!

Galactic silliness fills up the air,
As quirky star shapes begin to flare.
Our laughter erupts at the winks of fate,
Creating moments we can't replicate.

So let's sketch memories on the starlit floor,
With crayons of stardust, who could ask for more?
In this whimsical dance of fleeting dreams,
We play amongst beams and frolic in streams!

Stardust Wanderers

In space they zoom, all wild and free,
Two silly stars just sipping tea.
They giggle and dance on a comet's tail,
Waving at planets, leaving a trail.

The moon jumps in, claims it's a dance,
But tripping on asteroids ruins the chance.
Sunbeams are laughing, a cosmic jest,
These stardust buddies are truly the best.

Each twinkling wink holds a secret plan,
Making black holes jump, oh, what a jam!
With meteor showers, they splash about,
Silly stardust wanderers, dancing without a doubt.

Through starry nights where giggles soar,
They'll prank the Martians forevermore.
In a universe sweet, where chuckles await,
Sipping stardust tea, oh, what a fate!

Celestial Echoes

Echoes of laughter bounce through the sky,
Bouncing off planets as they whirl by.
A dodo bird winks from a quasar's glow,
"Hey, is that Earth?" they chortle below.

Twinkling lights with a flair for the fun,
Gallop through zodiacs, they just love to run.
Each comet a clown in a cosmic parade,
While Jupiter chuckles, its rings unafraid.

Saturn's proud voice booms out in delight,
"Thanks for the ruckus, it's quite a sight!"
Galactic parties with nebulae drinks,
Drifting on joy, they do silly clinks.

So next time you gaze at the night's quilted flair,
Know the echoing giggles of those dancing up there.
In the cosmic carnival, where humor looks great,
The sky's full of jesters, who simply can't wait!

The Cosmic Labyrinth

In a twisted maze where stars like to play,
A snail in a rocket shouts, "This is cray!"
Round and round in a spiral they go,
Singing to aliens, putting on a show.

A wacky black hole swirls in delight,
Sneaking up on comets with giggles at night.
"Hey, you can't catch me!" shouts one jovial comet,
But the black hole just laughs with a cosmic sonnet.

Through wormholes and bends, these jokes just unfold,
With Saturn's rings laughing, a sight to behold.
Each turn in the maze holds a new cosmic plea,
Jokes ricochet off starry glee.

So if you should wander where starlight can shine,
Remember these jokers, they're all doing fine.
In a labyrinth huge, where humor ignites,
Dance through the cosmos with pure, twinkling lights!

Whispers of the Galaxy

In the quiet of space, whispers fly high,
A giggle from Venus winks with a sigh.
"Why did Mars blush?" it playfully sings,
"Because it saw Earth wearing those rings!"

Across the vastness, a chuckle takes flight,
As stars share gossip under the moonlight.
Neptune, quite cheeky, lends a sly smirk,
As Saturn declares, "I'm the king of this work!"

With comets as jesters, antics abound,
Each supernova bursts with laughter profound.
In the whispers of skies where the wacky do roam,
Jokes echo through light-years, crafting a home.

So peek at the heavens when the night's just right,
And listen for giggles that twinkle bright.
For within each star, and in every ray,
Are whispers of joy in the cosmic ballet!

Voyage through the Starry Abyss

In a rocket fueled by soda pop,
I zigzag through the cosmos, non-stop.
My GPS has taken quite a break,
It shows a path made of ice-cream cake.

Bumping into asteroids with a laugh,
One looked like grandpa, what a gaffe!
I offered him a snack from the stash,
He just sighed and said, "Where's the crash?"

Jupiter's storms have pizza pies,
I snag a slice while munching on fries.
Hey, look! A comet with googly eyes,
Chasing it feels just like a surprise!

The Earth's just a dot, or so they say,
But I've found a planet where cows just sway.
With a moo that echoes through the night,
I ride my space llama, what a sight!

Forgotten Tales of the Universe

Once heard of a star that danced a jig,
It tripped on a nebula, oh so big!
With sparkles and twirls, it slipped and spun,
Said, "I'll show you how to have some fun!"

The black holes caught a game of tag,
But never caught the comet, what a drag.
It zipped and zoomed, just like a sprite,
Shouting, "Catch me quick! I'm outta sight!"

An alien chef makes spaghetti from light,
Twirling it up, oh what a sight!
Sauce made of gas and meatballs of stars,
Dinner served in shiny, spaceship jars.

And under the moons, where laughter reigns,
I met a creature with purple veins,
Told tales of planets made of cheese,
I sampled each one with jubilant ease!

Chasing the Celestial Tide

On a surfboard made of starlit dreams,
I ride the waves of cosmic beams.
The Milky's milking a colorful cow,
"Hold on tight!" I shout, but where's my pow?

Galaxies whirl like ball gowns in space,
I spin in circles—oh what a race!
Dodging asteroids like flying frisbees,
With giggles echoing in the cosmic breeze.

A space whale breaching, splashing blue goo,
It slid right by with a honking hello!
I offered it jelly from my pantry stash,
It gargled back, "I prefer my hash!"

With moons as my friends, we sing in the night,
Jamming on stars that feel just right.
Who knew the cosmos could throw such a bash?
With dance moves so wild, we make quite the clash!

Driftwood Among the Stars

I found a piece of driftwood so rare,
It whispered secrets of cosmic fare.
"Polka-dots are in, don't you know?"
I laughed and asked, "Was that from a show?"

Stars play hide-and-seek in the blue,
One winked at me, said, "What's up with you?"
I offered it a soda, it took a sip,
"Not bad for a journey on a long trip!"

Black holes are geese, honking away,
Chasing their tails in a bizarre ballet.
I joined the parade with my driftwood pal,
Floating along with a smirk and a howl.

And as the sun sets on this galactic spree,
I ponder the wonders that could be me.
With giggles and pranks I'll forever stay,
In this zany world, forever I'll play!

Timeless sojourn in the Cosmos

In a rocket made of cheese,
I zoom past planets with ease.
They wave their rings, I laugh and shout,
"Is that a comet or just a sprout?"

My spaceship has no GPS,
Just guesses and a slight distress.
Stars do a jig, then fade away,
I think I'm getting lost today.

I meet a Martian, he's a hoot,
Wearing funky alien boots.
We toast to stars, a cosmic fling,
His dance moves? Quite the interesting thing!

Asteroids dodge like sprightly friends,
While space whales sing, the fun never ends.
Through solar winds, my laughter flies,
In this mad chase, we're all astromites.

Embracing the Astral Void

I tumbled through a black hole's gate,
Thought I saw my past, but it was fate.
A chicken crossed on a comet's tail,
I honked the horn, we set to sail.

Galaxies twirl like dizzy tops,
While planets cook up cosmic chops.
I lost my sandwich; I lost my keys,
Hey, who stole my space-time breeze?

Neptune twirled in pinwheel dance,
While aliens begged for one more chance.
We swapped our jokes and puns and tales,
But who will pay our interstellar sails?

In the void, I found my groove,
As meteors jump and stars do move.
With laughter echoing through the space,
I guess I'll stay, it's quite the place!

Celestial Odyssey

Traveling fast, like super glue,
I mixed up Venus with someone new.
She called me out on my silly blunder,
And we both laughed, oh what a wonder!

Floating past a giant moon,
I tripped on stardust—caught a tune.
It sounded sweet, like candy rain,
And soon I danced, forgetting my pain.

The sun wore glasses, oh what a sight,
As comets boogied in pure delight.
I stuck my tongue out at a red planet,
It winked back, said, "You're quite the man, it!"

Each star was high-fiving in rhythm,
As I twirled 'round with brave optimism.
In this cosmic jest, I found my sway,
I'll never tire of this wild ballet!

Starlit Soliloquy

I scribbled notes on a shooting star,
Hoping it'd hitch a ride from afar.
But it zoomed by with a giggling trail,
I shouted, "Hey! Don't leave me to flail!"

Clouds made shapes, of cats and fish,
I swore I saw a cosmic dish.
When stars collide, do they share a laugh?
Or just mumble under their bright autograph?

Pluto threw a party; I was late,
Had to dodge some asteroids—what a fate!
When I arrived, it was quite the sight,
Space socks dancing left and right!

With every twinkle and quirk in sight,
I embraced the absurd, the pure delight.
In this starlit play, I found my say,
Cosmic comedy to brighten my day!

www.ingramcontent.com/pod-product-compliance
Lightning Source LLC
Chambersburg PA
CBHW071834160426
43209CB00003B/300